DID YOU SURVIVE 2020?

Revisit the events of 2020, realize your role in thc universe, claim your luck and empower yourself to win over any disaster

DR. EESHA RAJPUT

eesharajput84@gmail.com

ABOUT THE AUTHOR

Dr. Eesha Rajput is a radiologist by profession and wife, mother, author, counsellor by occupation. After finishing medical school at the prestigious Armed Forces Medical College, Pune, she pursued her postgraduate training in Radiodiagnosis and Imaging. She authored four successful books on Radiology that are an absolute essential for the post graduate training programme.

Alongside she developed interest in humanity and has authored this book centered on COVID 19 crisis, empowering us to prepare ourselves for any disaster or calamity. This is the first book in the series "Wholesome Health".

To know more about the upcoming releases and read blogs from the author, the reader is requested to visit the website www.eesharajput.com. Find her and shower your love on facebook, linkedin, Instagram, medium.com and twitter.

DISCLAIMER

All the events, names and circumstances mentioned in this book are fictional and any resemblance to any person living or dead is purely coincidental.

Author's note

What is normal? Normal is when events repeat themselves in a premeditated manner over and over again, days after days, weeks after weeks, years after years. Normal is predictable, normal is monotonous. But, normal is also safe. Never before in my life at the ripe age of thirty-five, had I longed for a normal monotonous day so much.

The COVID 19 pandemic changed the definition of the word 'normal'. Here is a story of an Indian family in California who struggled hard and was faced with innumcrable challenges during the pandemic.

The story and events are related as they happened over the months of 2020.

But, even after facing seemingly world-ending situations, life goes on. The human race, homo sapiens sapiens, have an indomitable spirit, an insatiable thirst to EXIST. We will conquer this too and rise from the ashes again.

As we prepare to welcome the new year, let us connect, realize, and imbibe this, that we existed during COVID 19, we survived the worst pandemic that humanity has ever gone through, and put our best efforts to fight the pandemic. Let us be proud of ourselves. Let us celebrate love, life, and work through COVID, through 2020. Let us celebrate the new 'normal'.

<u>Gratitude</u>

I take this opportunity to thank my family, my husband Cdr PK Singh, and my children, for sticking by me through this pandemic. How else would I survive this?

I thank the Almighty for giving me a chance, to live through COVID 19, to be able to tell tales, to the next generation.

I thank nature for the simple joys of life which I will never take for granted, again.

I thank you, the reader, for bestowing on this book your most important possession, your time.

Let us embark on this journey together, hand in hand, "Did You Survive 2020?", the first book in "Wholesome Health series".

Chapter 1

The incident/accident

Institute of Geosciences Resource Evaluation
Laboratory
27 Oct, 2019 0200hrs

The lab had an eerie feel to it at this time of the night. There were no sounds, absolute silence. Nature was in deep sleep. But, this was Xang Jin's favorite time to work. 56 years young, Xang had dedicated his whole life to microbiology and virology. He was a revered academician, elusive to the external world. His morning, days, and nights were all spent only in the lab or his office which was located on the secret floor of this fifty-four floor towering building.

In this institute, world-level advanced scientific and virological research was done. This lab was jointly funded by the Chinese and United Nations (UN) authorities – a major contribution was from the United State of America as well.

The Chief of the institute, popularly called "The Hawk", was a hard-core administrator and a military-minded person. Under the garbs of research and development, this lab was also dedicated to the ulterior motives of developing biological weapons. World War III would not be fought by the armies. It would be a very different scenario – whenever that happens – not "if".

Xang reported only to the Chief. The only other person who had access to Xang's words was Page, Xang's assistant of two years. Page had graduated from the University of California, a reputed organization. Being a marvelous student, she managed to grab the opportunity to work under Dr. Xang. Page was in awe of Xang's academic persona.

In the wee hours of the night, page noticed something unusual. Xang got up from the study with the key to the underground storage facility in one hand and on the other hand, he was carrying a vial, and he was "smiling'. Xang and smile – that was not a common occurrence together.

"The Chief will be happy", Xang thought as he entered the corridor to the storage facility.

0400 hours

Two hours had passed after Xang went to the storage facility. He had not returned – very unusual. The temperatures and radiation limits in the storage facility allowed a person to stay in only for 15-20 minutes, 30 minutes at the maximum, even with level 4 designed virological suits and breathing apparatus.

Page decided to check in on Xang. After meeting Xang, she will call it a day, she thought. The day had been tiring with all statistical calculations, documentation, and data analysis job given to her by Xang.

She ritually donned her virological suite. This suite provided a safe atmosphere to protect the wearer from any viruses in the ambient air. It was specifically designed for high-level virological research centers like this one. All viral prototype samples from smallpox to influenza were stored here. And no one would like to get exposed to such a nuisance professionally or accidentally.

On entering the storage facility, Page was taken aback. Xang was lying on the floor. His oxygen tubing was disrupted. The vial he was carrying was lying on the floor too, cracked, and some greenish fluid leaking out of it. It was a grade IV emergency – a biological hazard leak situation. The situation was much higher than the CODE RED in hospitals. It could bring a calamity of indeterminate proportions. Page was frozen. She didn't know what to do. She dragged Xang's heavy body out of the storage facility and closed the triple door entry behind her. In the process, some more fluid from the vial came out and spread along the stairs and lift nearby.

Gaining her senses back, she did what she was trained for. She pressed the HIGH-LEVEL EMERGENCY button. The phone ringed. Worriedly sick, Page blattered whatever had happened on the phone.

"It will be taken care of." said the voice at the other end.

In the next two to three minutes, what followed was a scene right from sci-fi movies. Full virological suit-clad, in orange and black colors, people appeared out of nowhere. Few carried Dr. Xang's lifeless body out of the building with strict precautions. Few swept the storage facility, lift, and stairs with devices straight out of the movie "Matrix". Two of them started decontaminating Page as if she was an object.

The nightmare was over, but, the consequences were not. For the next 14 days, Page was kept in an isolation facility and her blood samples and vitals were assessed daily. Every day approximately 10ml of her blood was drawn out for various tests, details of which were not revealed to her. Even after several requests to speak to the Chief, Page did not receive any communication.

After 14 days of isolation, when she rejoined the lab, she found a letter on her table from the HR department. It stated that her services were no longer required, the contract was terminated and she may return to California. The flight tickets were enclosed – the flight was scheduled after four hours.

This was absurd. No reasons were given. Nobody even bothered to speak to her. Xang's office was now occupied by a bald man Dr. Jao. It seemed like Xang's complete existence had vanished after the incident. Suddenly, a shadow appeared behind her. Page was escorted out of the building. Page felt humiliated. She boarded

the flight to California and vouched never to
return to China.

As the flight took off, a phone call was made to
the Chief, "She left."

Chapter 2

The introduction

"Om burbhuvah svah tat saviturvarenyam bhargodevasya dhimahi dhiyo yo na prachodayat" - Gayatri Mantra

"Svaha", said Panditji.
"Svaha", everybody repeated after him.
It was an auspicious day. Angad was finally getting engaged.

Angad was a modern age boy, educated, well-groomed, earning a handsome salary in a multinational consultancy firm. An enthusiast at heart. Adventurous. Risk-taking. An eligible bachelor in every sense. All these qualities also made a mark in his love life. Throughout his years at senior secondary and college, he had multiple love interests. Shailaja had lost count of them. However, the topic of marriage had remained elusive to him. Probably, the failed relationship of his parents had left an unseen scar in his amygdala. Shailaja feared for the possibility that Angad may never let himself find "the one".

Angad met Shruti during a boring meeting.
Their eyes met and gave signals to each other to
meet outside. Shruti excused herself to attend a
call. Angad dropped some coffee on his shirt,
apparently by mistake, and moved out for a
quick wash.

"Aah, what a relief!" said Shruti.
"How are you connected to the AEW
consultancy?" asked Angad.
"I am assistant to the financial advisor."
"Hmmm, finances department."
"Yes..."
"Boring ....."
"Why?" asked Shruti, surprised.
"People in finances worry only about money.
They are not interesting people."
"I would like to differ."
"I am sure."
"Either you can stick to your biased views or you
can find some new facts."
"New facts – that would be good. How about a
coffee break after the meeting?"

They met for coffee after the meeting and that
was followed by many more – at coffee shops,
restaurants, walkways, and later at Shruti's
rented apartment. After five months of 'getting

to know each other', Angad brought Shruti home
to meet Shailaja.

Shailaja was overjoyed. Shruti was an
independent girl, fairly good looking, smart,
impressive, and most importantly, Indian. All
along the past few years, she had been thinking,
what if Angad wants to marry an American girl,
how would she handle the situation?

Shailaja was a naïve Indian girl, well educated,
ahead of her times. She was kind at heart and
thought that the world around her was also
simple and kind just like her. But, fate had sour
plans for her. She was married into a Brahmin
family and like all young girls, she also looked
forward to a 'happy ever after' – which never
happened. Initial differences with her husband
over petty issues turned into recurrent fights
and assaults. Finally, tired of the bruises and
bleeds, Shailaja left home and escaped to the US
with the help of her maternal uncle. Divorce
papers followed. She never looked back.

Unaware then, she was carrying a small life in
her womb and a few months later she was
blessed with a baby boy – Angad. Angad was the
reason for her existence, the apple of her eyes.

Her whole life revolved around him. Angad's innocent smile made all hard days seem easy. Her husband never tried to contact them. Scarred for life, she could never find love again.

Shailaja had a BSc nursing degree from India. When she came to the US, the initial years were tough. Angad was small. She used to work two jobs to support her bills, morning as a babysitter and evenings as a waitress. She earned enough to save some for her further training. Her employers, the Boyers, were benevolent enough to allow her to bring Angad during babysitting. After Angad turned three and started preschool, Shailaja enrolled herself in MSc nursing. Boyers supported her with filling correct forms, opening a bank account, and applying for social security schemes.

Years passed. The once petite girl, with a newborn to support, transformed into a smart dynamic Nursing matron at a reputed hospital in California, the Healers Hospital. She was a force to reckon with at the hospital. Even young trainees found it difficult to match her energy levels. In-charge of managing duties of nursing personnel in OT, ER, wards, NICU, and labor rooms, she was practically the backbone of the hospital. It was a demanding job. But, Shailaja did it with total commitment. All these years of relentless work had taken its toll on her health and she suffered frequent panic attacks – she controlled it herself with the help of few medications.

Chapter 3

Day Zero

17 November, 2019

South China Morning Post – a Chinese daily newspaper carried a report of a 55-year-old man, a resident of Hubei province in China, infected with respiratory disease.
This and a cluster of cases occurred till Dec 8, 2019, but, no information about this disease was shared with the world.

Near the end of December 2019, the Chinese authorities declared an epidemic that began with a cluster of cases in an animal market in Wuhan province of China. Whistleblowers in the medical community stated that this was a novel disease with an unknown pathogen and high transmission rates. Dozens of patients were being admitted with this pneumonia-like illness of unknown cause. The causative organism being novel, the treatment protocols were not in place and chaos resulted. The patient presented with cough, fever, respiratory problems, and

desaturation. Some of them would just faint
with no alerting feature. None of the cases,
however, were confirmed to be "patient zero". So
the epidemic investigations were not yielding
any results.

The numbers increased from 27 on 15
December, to 60 on 20 December, to 381 on 1
January 2020. The new year came with a ticking
time bomb – a calamity of unknown proportions
– of which the world knew nothing about.

Dr. Zhang Jixian, a doctor from Hubei
Provincial Hospital of Integrated Chinese and
Western Medicine, informed Chinese health
authorities that the new disease was a novel
coronavirus.

According to WHO, the first coronavirus case
was documented on December 8, 2020. The
global body failed to rack the disease itself and
relied on member nations to provide their
information.

In contradictory documents, a report published
in the medical journal Lancet, logged the earliest
patient as early as December 1 in Jinyintan
Hospital in Wuhan, while doctors in Wuhan say

that they weren't aware of the disease until late December.

Midway through January, Wuhan health authorities claimed that there were only 41 confirmed cases of coronavirus.

WHO – China Joint Mission on COVID 19 – Press Conference on 24 February 2020.
The briefing was done by team leaders of the Joint Mission, Dr. Bruce Aylward, former Assistant Director-General of WHO and senior advisor to WHO Director-General and Dr. Liang Wanmian, Head of the expert panel of COVID 19 Response of China National Health Commission (NHC).
Following five points were brought out in the meeting:

1. Coronavirus is a novel virus of the coronaviridae family, related to SARS and MERS viruses. The disease caused by this coronavirus was termed COVID 19 for coronavirus disease 2019. Whole gene sequencing revealed that there were no obvious variations in strains of the virus in different parts of the world.

2. Epidemiological characteristics – the average age of the affected patient was 51 years, varying between 30-69 years.
3. Host – the primary host of the virus was unclear. Likely the host was bats, pangolin may also be an intermediate host.
4. Routes of transmission – transmission route was respiratory droplets and contact with surfaces contaminated by the virus. Familial clustering was identified due to close contact between family members.
5. Disease susceptibility – Since this was a novel disease, the whole of the population was susceptible to the virus. The proportion of mild, moderate, and severe cases was 80%, 16%, and 4% respectively. It was unclear if asymptomatic carriers also spread the disease.

Chapter 4

The Guests

The event was lavish. It was Valentine's day theme party on February 14th, 2020 for the special day of Angad and Shruti. The event had a dream-like feel. Love was in the air. The venue appeared like an old fashioned American inspired backyard shindig. Trees were decorated with streamers, miniflags with the message "Angad and Shruti are hitched" adorned the centerpieces on the tables. Artistically decorated potato salad, chilled beer, and Indian cuisine with American tadka was the layout. Ghazals by Ghulam Ali stirred the atmosphere till the ring exchange ceremony, after which, the new couple and their friends danced away the night on the tune of Bollywood masala songs.

Shailaja had ensured that her son's engagement was an event that the people in the community would remember. Although she had shifted to California decades back, the Indian mindset of showing off at grand events was secretly ingrained in her too.

For her, having gone through the turmoils of life on her own terms, having raised Angad with celebratory Indian values and now his engagement to an Indian girl were factors enough to call in for a grand celebration.

Shailaja wanted Angad's wedding, planned in May, to be grander than the engagement. Talks had already begun with Shruti's parents to ask Panditji and find a 'shubh muhurat' so that things could be planned meticulously.

Among family and friends in a happy atmosphere, Angad and Shruti exchanged rings with each other. "Congratulations!!" shouted everybody. The looks in the couple's eyes betrothed their commitment to this relationship. Shailaja couldn't help but notice this moment and savored every bit of it. She deserved happiness.

Time for a fun photo. The photographer said, "Say cheese everybody..." and Shailaja ducked. Beads of perspiration appeared on her forehead. "Excuse me," she said and went to the washroom. Angad noticed and told everyone that she would be fine and others should just move on with the flow. He knew where she went. Shailaja quickly took out a tablet from her purse, gulped it with some water, and sat on the washroom floor, as she heard noises of pictures clicking outside.

The fear and anxiety never left her. The products of a broken relationship are not just two people – it is two broken people. The husband may or may not have moved on. But, with all the stress that she dealt with in her life, Shailaja lost something within. Her mind was scarred forever. Any situation of extreme emotions – happiness, sorrow, or excitement – used to precipitate such panic attacks. She was now accustomed to controlling them.

After all, she was the head nurse. No one should know. Else her hard-earned job would be in jeopardy. The circumstances in the hospital, OT, ER, were all high-pressure situations, that demanded increased mental agility. Her panic attack problem would be a problem if known to the HR department and administrators. Although Angad was earning well now, Shailaja considered her job as her independence, her priciest possession. She could not afford to lose

it at any cost – even if it sometimes caused
enough stress to precipitate the panic attacks.

There had been requests from many nursing
colleges for Shailaja to join as teaching staff. It
would be a stable job with a decent income
minus all the stress of managing work at a
hospital. Angad tried to convince her to change
gears. Her advancing age did not match with the
profile of the job she was doing. He wanted his
mother to be safe and happy – a doting son! But,
Shailaja would chuckle and say, "Abhi to main
jawan hoon. (I am still young)." And
conveniently decline all suggestions. She
celebrated her 50 years last year, but in her
mind, she was strong, agile, and could never be
subdued, again.

Among the people who attended the
engagement, Dev Arora was a prominent invitee.
He was the local sheriff, Indian origin, but his
forefathers had settled in America and now,
America was his motherland. He had strong
muscular shoulders, an authoritative stance, and
inquisitive eyes – eyes that were always looking
at things with suspicion. He was a family friend.
So, Angad's engagement was a happy occasion
for him to attend.

Dev's inquisitive eyes met Sandeep's for a second. Sandeep was Shailaja 'yes man', the driver who doubled up as helper, caretaker, sometimes even cook. Betting and gambling were his weaknesses. Somehow, he could not tolerate Dev's intriguing looks and went aside to distribute sweets to the departing guests.

The last one to leave was Mr. Patel, a Gujju from India. Due to his lisping tone, he was mocked by one and all in his family and also by friends at school, and later college. So, he dropped out of college and cajoled his father to send him to America to study. Father was a wealthy businessman and thought that Patel would add value quotient to his business with his foreign degree. Patel came to America, did small jobs, to begin with, got some ideas, and opened an Indian saree shop. It rocked with the migrant population there. Other smaller businesses followed like restaurants and soon he earned his way to success.

Forty-two now, he never married. His heart had a soft corner for Shailaja. Although, he could never express himself. He was scared of being rejected and spoiling the beautiful friendship he shared with Shailaja. He loved Angad like his own son. Angad was also quite close to Patel. Their weekend sessions of fishing, cycling, mountaineering were a routine that both of them punctually attended to. Patel was very happy that Angad was getting married. Shruti seemed to be the perfect match for him. And they loved each other a lot – that everyone could tell.

All in all, things were going on well, actually much better than WELL!!!

Chapter 5

The Beginning of the Mayhem

WHO site alert – Jan 2020

The Director-General of WHO declared the novel coronavirus as PHEIC (Public Health Emergency of International concern) – WHO's highest level of alarm.
At that time, there were 998 confirmed cases of coronavirus in 18 countries outside China and 4 countries reported community transmission.

Excerpts from an article in the New England Journal of Medicine published on January 31, 2020, at NETM.org.

This report described the epidemiological and clinical features of the first case of coronavirus nCoV infection confirmed in the US.

On December 31, 2019, China reported a cluster of cases of pneumonia in people associated with the Hunan seafood wholesale market in Wuhan, Hubei province in China. As of January 30, the number of cases in China was approximately seven thousand.

On January 19, a 35-year-old man presented to an emergency clinic at Snohomish County, Washington, with a four-day history of cough and fever. He had put on a mask in the waiting room. During the examination, he revealed that he had returned to Washington after visiting his family in Wuhan, China. He stated that he had seen a health alert from the US Centre for Disease Control and Prevention (CDC) about the novel coronavirus outbreak in China and because of his symptoms and recent travel history, he decided to see a health care provider.

His vitals – pulse, blood pressure, was stable. He had increased respiratory rate and decreased spO2 (a measurement to ascertain oxygen saturation in the blood). He tested negative for Influenza A and B. CDC was notified. The patient denied spending any time at the Huanan seafood market and his contact history was nil significant. Specimen for testing were collected by following CDC guidelines. It included blood for serum and nasopharyngeal swab specimen.

The patient was sent to 14 days of strict home isolation with active monitoring by the local health department.

On January 20, 2020, the reports confirmed that the patient is positive for 2019-nCoV by real-time reverse transcriptase-polymerase chain reaction (rRT-PCR) test.

The patient was admitted to an airborne isolation unit at Providence Regional Medical Center for clinical observation. The health care workers there followed all recommendations for the prevention of contact, droplet, and airborne diseases, along with eye protection.

On admission, the patient had a dry cough and nausea. Day 2-5 of the illness were largely uneventful and treatment offered was primarily supportive.

Day 6-8, the patient started showing a drop in oxygen saturation. Chest radiograph revealed bilateral lower zone ill-defined infiltrates. Oxygen supplementation was given with nasal canula at 2L per minute. Antibiotics were started. Also, an institutional antiviral regimen with intravenous Remdesivir (a novel nucleotide analog prodrug in development) was implemented.

The patient started improving on day 10 and was largely stable on day 12. He was discharged on day 14 of admission and advised for a further 14 day home isolation.

All his contacts were traced and tested.

This was just the beginning. What followed was complete chaos. The number of cases of coronavirus started increasing exponentially. The disease was new, everyone was susceptible, no cure was known, transmission rates were high and there was no vaccine. The recipe for the end of humanity was cooked and ready. It was coming to take us all, sparing none.

As of March 4th, 2020, cases of COVID had been spread in 77 countries.

WHO launched the Strategic Preparedness and Response Plan for COVID 19 aimed to:
- Slow and stop transmission, prevent outbreaks, and delay spread.
- Provide optimized care for all patients, especially those that were seriously ill.

- Minimize the impact of the epidemic on health systems, social services, and economic activity.

Four transmission scenarios were defined for COVID 19:
- Countries with no cases (no cases)
- Countries with one or more cases, imported or locally detected (sporadic cases)
- Countries experiencing cases clusters in time, geographic location and /or common exposure (cluster of cases)
- Countries experiencing larger outbreaks of local transmission (community transmission)

Chapter 6

Lockdown

First stay at home order in the US.

"California orders lockdown for state's 40 million residents." – Wall Street Journal, March 19th, 2020.

There is apprehension in the air.
Curfews, quarantines, stay at home orders were placed in many countries around the world. Measures were aimed to prevent further spread of SARS coronavirus 2 SARS-CoV2, which causes the disease COVID 19.

By April 2020, about half of the world's population was under lockdown with more than 3.9 billion people in more than 90 countries ordered to stay at home by their governments.

The WHO recommendation on curfews and lockdowns stated that these were short-term measures to reorganize, regroup, rebalance, redirect resources and protect health care workers, who were getting exhausted by the sheer volume of the illness. A balance had to be sought between restrictions and normal life. Normal life seemed like a distant dream for now. The long term response would consist of strict personal hygiene, contact tracing, and isolation of all patients.

In keeping with the government advised restrictions:
- All schools, colleges, universities, and educational institutions were closed till further orders.
- All shops were closed. Markets were closed. Only grocery shops and pharmaceutical shops were allowed to open, with severe time and social distancing protocols.
- All industries with the production of non-essential items were shut down.
- Recreational venues, stadiums, public places (museums, etc) were closed.
- Border closure took place. All international flights were canceled.
- Travel restrictions were placed and travel advisories were issued. People got

stranded in different parts of the world. Reaching hometown for a relative's funeral was also not possible due to the non-availability of means of travel.
- After traveling from one state to another, strict quarantine for 14 days had to be followed with testing regulations.
- Social distancing advisories were put in place. People were expected to maintain 6 feet distance between them at all public places.
- Wearing a face mask was mandatory in all public places.

These restrictions began in China and soon other countries like the US, UK, France, New Zealand, Spain, Vietnam, Italy - followed suit. By the end of April, around three-quarters of humanity was under total lockdown with severe restrictions.

Chapter 7

The effects

After the COVID 19 touched the shores of different countries in the world, the disease spread like wildfire. The number of cases overwhelmed the health care systems of even the biggest economies in the world.
There were death and sickness everywhere. The number of coffins was falling short. There was no place to bury the dead.

All news channels in all the parts of the world only carried the news related to coronavirus and suddenly, there was not much difference in your fate whether you belonged to a third world country or a developed nation. COVID 19 did not differentiate between the rich and the poor.

It was everywhere and the only topic of concern in the webinars worldwide. The world's top experts were at their wit's end trying to find solutions to limit the catastrophe.

WHO declared the COVID 19 disease as a pandemic on 11th March 2020.

Health care workers:

The pandemic placed health care professionals throughout the world in an unprecedented situation. These health care workers, also called CORONA WARRIORS, were at the frontline in COVID 19 pandemic response, and hence had the highest risk of infection. Hospital associated transmission was one of the most important routes of spread of the illness.

As far as professional duties were concerned, the health care workers had to put in practice the art of 'unlearn, relearn' like never before. New safety practices and regulations had to be followed like wearing a PPE (personal protective equipment – an overall that made you look like a snowman), face mask, face shield, double gloves, and eyeglasses. Managing patients after donning such paraphernalia was a daunting task. While wearing the PPE, one could not eat, drink or use the toilet, so, shift duties were limited to 4-6hours; but this time was also very difficult as you sweat profusely after wearing

PPE, just for even 10 minutes. Spending 4 hours in PPE was an inhumane request.

Added to this was the mental stress of long shift duties, distress related to patient's death, occupational burnout, social stigma. Fear of own safety, worries about family and children's health, childcare issues, fear of contracting the illness from patients – all the factors were leading to the crisis of health care workers reporting for duty.

<u>Police and security personnel:</u>

Lack of staff preparedness and education, limited provision of PPE, crisis counseling, and absence of vaccine – all this posed a serious challenge to the cornerstone of the fight with coronavirus – the police force.

Along with healthcare professionals, the police force was assigned with the distressing task of ensuring strict lockdown norms issued by the government and contact tracing and screening of cases. How to approach the fearful and uncooperative population and what steps the police should take to ensure security and

transmission prevention in the community –
was a million-dollar question.

People said that their freedom and basic rights
were denied if they were told to wear a mask in
public places. Protests began asking for freedom
and the removal of lockdowns. Such large
gatherings further risked the rise of COVID 19
cases.

Freedom means the ability to act or change
without constraint. So, you should use your
freedom to make conscious decisions that are
beneficial to you and the universe. Just sticking
to a fixed idea that not following any rules and
regulations is freedom, that is detrimental.

Police had to ensure social distancing at shops
and grocery stores, hospitals, and testing
centers. They also had to provide security and
smooth conduct of periodical lockdowns.

While discharging their duties, many police
personnel contracted the infection themselves
and laid their lives in the service of the nation.

The fear for the life of self and families was
looming large in the minds of all workers

enrolled in emergency services like hospitals, police, water, electricity, sanitation, defense, and paramilitary forces.

<u>Business and entrepreneurship</u>

Many businesses suffered huge losses – industries, aviation sector, hospitality, and tourism – these services were on the verge of complete bankruptcy. Millions of people in the private sector were rendered jobless.

More than 70% of startups had to terminate full-time employee contracts since the start of the COVID 19 pandemic. As sources of finance dry up, more than 40% of ventures will fall into the "Red zone" with only enough cash to survive three months or less of normal operations.

Small businesses suffered huge losses. But governments started working overtime to support local ecosystems with proposals like rescue financial packages.

Online, work-from-home options saw a booming rise.
Alternative entrepreneurship has seen an unprecedented rise. Automotive companies have

now been forced to pivot into manufacturing ventilators.
Clothes and sartorial craftsmen have ventured into mask design and protective equipment. Conferences have given way to webinars, con-calls, and virtual meets.

These changes made us realize that many things about which we fret daily actually do not matter that much. There are alternative ways of doing things. Adjustment at every level is possible. You just need to have an open mindset to keep things working. The show must go on.

If a software designer, who happens to be a lady with a small child, does not report for work one day stating that her child is sick, the boss throws a tantrum saying that such a lackadaisical attitude will not work, it will take her nowhere. She should have made arrangements for someone to look after her child etc, etc. Whereas in the scenario that we witnessed in 2020, almost all the companies had shifted to work from home culture to save their employees from the pandemic. Major decisions like company takeovers were taken on web calls. So you see, it is not that difficult. Had the ill-tempered boss allowed the lady to attend work online for a few days till the child gets well, she could have contributed to the productivity of the firm while attending to her familial responsibility. Women are superb at multitasking. I can assure you that from personal experience.

So that's what 2020 made us realize. Be adaptable. Be compassionate. All of us have bad days. It is just that today is not your turn. But who knows? The game may change overnight. So, brace yourself. Be kind. Kindness comes back in varied forms.

Schools and education:

Schools were closed, but, education did not stop. Soon, the education pattern turned into an online approach. The mode was technology-intensive and yes, this was not an option in poorer countries of the world. But everywhere else, the lucky ones could attend online classes. The role of a teacher had changed overnight. They were expected to design interactive presentations, involve children in online classes, and be the silver lining in the dark clouds of coronavirus.

Enjoyable days:

In some parts of the world, people enjoyed the lockdown with indoor games, binge-watching shows on Netflix, ordering delicacies for home delivery – in short, having a lifetime of a vacation.

Laborers:

True, this was a bad time to be poor. In other parts of the world, there were daily wage workers and laborers in industries who lost their occupation overnight due to lockdown norms and that too, for an indefinite period.

In many parts of India, there was an exodus of workers from one part of the country to another, risking a high rise in corona cases.

Bankruptcy:

Companies both large and small were succumbing to the effects of corona and filing for bankruptcy. Most viable companies and those that could be saved were teetering on an edge. Reforms in systems were the need of the hour – increasing budgets, relaxing tight deadlines, were few to mention.

People panicked everywhere. In April 2020, 22 million Americans filed unemployment claims. 58% of Americans in a survey by Trans Union's Online Poll of 3000 US adults, said that they had lost their jobs and were unable to pay rents and bills and could not buy essential groceries due to lockdown and unemployment crisis.

In a study published in the American Journal of public health, symptoms of anxiety, depression, and somatization were more in unemployed persons as compared to employed people. Even suicide rates were higher in the unemployed lot. All these facts were put to the litmus test in 2020, and yes, they were proved right with each passing month.

Chapter 8

Patel's plight

Patel with his sheer hard work and enterprise had managed to set up his Indian

sarees business and restaurants. These were the source for his revenue, his daily living. For the last eight months, all non-essential shops were closed. Non-essential industries were either closed or working with 25% strength. It was difficult to generate enough money to pay salaries to all workers. He had to show red slip to a few of his men. It was a very saddening state.

Marriages, functions, get-togethers were words from a different reality. Events at which lavish clothes would be required were not happening. The need for grand and lavish had disappeared. All those people now longed for were simple normal things in life like the freedom to go out for a walk or exercise in the gym.

In such a scenario, the business community was incurring huge losses and Patel was no different. Patel was under a lot of mental stress. Slightly weak in the matters of heart and mind right from his childhood, with no support in view, he took refuge in his friend and one-sided love interest, Shailaja.

"I don't know what to do. All these years, although I was away from home and my family in India, I never felt so lonely. I was busy with my work. My routine was set. That gave me happiness, a reason to wake up in the morning. These days, I have no drive, no enthusiasm to live through. It is so lonely. I don't go out. I don't meet anyone. No trips to the shop or restaurant. I miss my family. They are happy for me that I could achieve success in California, but I guess, I am not happy for myself."

Shailaja, with her tired eyes, which had seen nothing but death and sickness all day, gave a loving look to Patel and said, "Talk to them. Give a call to your friends and family back home. There is no other way to stay sane. We are going through a calamity – the effects of which are deep within. We don't know how long it is going to continue. Find out about your loved ones.

They may also be feeling low and wanting to speak to you. Go ahead. Open up. Lockdown is only for physical forms, not emotions and relations. Keep in touch."

"Good advice." Patel thought. Only Shailaja could offer such simple solutions to seemingly unending issues.

Although, he very well knew that she was not able to hold on too well. Sometimes, he wished that they could speak to each other in words all that their eyes said to each other. It would probably make this world a better place to live in. Such was the power of love.

Not today.

"I will call home." He said and left.

The pandemic made us realize the importance of friends and communication. Friendship increases life expectancy and our chances to survive difficult situations. It helps us to survive. Numerous studies have mentioned the release of neurobiological hormones like endorphins and oxytocin when we deeply communicate.

Friendship makes us feel good and confident about ourselves. It helps us to get over a crisis, plan the future, and move ahead together.

Friendship is an evolutionary trait. It has found mention in the Indian epic - The Ramayana, where Lord Ram befriends Sugriva and Hanuman to find his lost wife, Sita. The friendship of Lord Ram with Hanuman is the subject of eternal trust and deep solace which they find in each other's presence.

Chapter 9

<u>Hydroxychloroquine</u>

At the international level, multiple measures were being taken to ameliorate the effects of the coronavirus pandemic.

Along with treating patients, epidemiological studies were being carried out to identify clusters and contain them effectively.

Few people, however, did not listen to security personnel and flouted lockdown norms publicly.

Medical trials were going on to identify some cure for this new coronavirus.

Hydroxychloroquine, an antimalarial drug emerged as one of the contenders in the quest for coronavirus remedy. It was published in Lancet – an accomplished medical journal – that hydroxychloroquine could significantly help in the treatment of COVID 19. This report led all countries to start the production and import of hydroxychloroquine.

It was considered the magic drug by everyone. Sales were limited by the government. Export to other countries was stopped. India was emerging as the new pharmaceutical giant with a maximum production of hydroxychloroquine and ready to export it to the USA.

Accreditation of investigating labs was another issue. There were a limited number of laboratories that could run the RT-PCR test for novel coronavirus.

Testing for COVID 19 could be done by two methods:

- First was RTPCR. In this method, the RNA from the virus was extracted from nasopharyngeal swabs. This RNA was converted to DNA by reverse transcriptase enzyme and amplified millions of times by polymerase chain reaction (PCR) method. This is a very sensitive test used to diagnose individual cases, for contact tracing, and for containing outbreaks.
- The second test is the rapid antigen test. The antigen is the part of the pathogen that elicits an immune response. Antigen

tests identify proteins from the viral surface, the surface spikes of the COVID virus. Rapid tests are less sensitive and are useful for screening patients in emergencies.

Other methods like antibody levels can be used to assess disease prevalence and infection rates.

The investigation, treatment, and sequelae were all evolving, as was the disease itself.

What do you do when you don't know what will happen?
A famous quote says "My unknown future is in the hands of the all-knowing GOD".
When you don't know what lies ahead, when you are scared of what lies ahead, you survive with faith. Faith that it is not in your hands that things will go as planned. You can control the process, you cannot control the outcome. Despite this, you must believe that there is a plan for your purpose in this universe, you must believe in that and yourself, no matter what. You have to notice the discomfort, the emptiness, the calamity, and still stand undeterred. It is then that you will witness the light at the end of the

road, you will witness your life, your purpose in this universe, your claim at your luck.

Chapter 10

Shailaja's secret

Salaries to healthcare workers were not paid by the government and private institutions for a long time due to the economic crisis. In many parts of the world, the nursing staff staged quiet protests about their difficult state. But, working under the Hippocratic oath meant working always, even without pay, if your patient's life was in danger.

Anyone with a minimum experience in the healthcare sector was placed in COVID duties.

Shailaja was facing a lot of issues in managing duties and placing people on work shifts in COVID wards. No matter how much she motivated her staff, in her heart she knew that she was putting them in harm's way and the advice she was giving them fell on deaf ears. There was death everywhere, all around the hospital.

Nurses and doctors were forced to take life and death decisions every day. Due to the limited number of ventilators, sometimes they had to remove respiratory support of old age patients to give a relatively younger patient a chance to live. But, do the elderly not have the right to live? Are their lives less worth than others? All of us will become elderly at some point in our lives. Where are ethics and duty in denying ventilator support to a patient? All these questions and more ruffled the minds of those on duty every day. And, it was not easy to remain calm under such chaos.

People left the hospital with mixed feelings. There were many whose relatives improved, became healthy, and were discharged from the hospital. But, then some lost their loved ones to the disease. In such situations, grief mostly takes over your wisdom and decision making. And in a fury of grief, many people abused or behaved improperly with the hospital staff.

The hospital staff usually is very helpful and compassionate. But, their soft skills, good behavior, and compassion should not be taken for granted. They are also human beings, they have feelings. They have been dealing with nothing but death since the pandemic began. So, if anyone needs some encouraging words and a pat on the back, it is them. We must not forget what other people are going through even if we are overwhelmed with our problems.

 Shailaja suffered multiple panic attacks during her COVID responsibilities, a few of which were witnessed by the hospital staff. She was administered anxiolytics by the doctors, but the word was out. Shailaja could no more be trusted with high-pressure jobs like hospital matron in charge. Her close aides told her that hospital management was looking for her replacement. But, due to the COVID scenario, they were not getting a suitable candidate.

Shailaja knew that it was just a matter of time before they did and then she would be asked to resign or work under the new matron. She hated this feeling. But, she knew it was coming.

"CODE RED" in OT. She heard the announcement on the speaker. Getting rid of her thoughts, she ran towards the announcement room to send reinforcement to OT, while looking at the shift schedule displayed on the notice board in the corridor.

Rumors were another plot spoiling medium in this pandemic. Rumour refers to a piece of information that may or may not be true, but people are talking about it. Rumors do not need doors and windows to move. They don't even touch lips. They just fly. Some people are strong enough not to listen to them or not get affected by them. But most of the others, the lesser mortals, who do not possess such amazing abilities of no-concern fall prey to such gimmicks and harm themselves or their happiness over such insignificant issues. Mental strength and agility are very important to survive rumors, more so during pandemics of the magnitude that we witnessed in 2020.

Chapter 11

Night Queen

Night Queen was the infamous place in the infamous neighborhood. It was a night club with all activities – booze, drugs, prostitution, betting, gambling, money laundering – all illegal activities that could happen used to occur here.

Sandeep was walking down the deserted road. At the end of the road, he took an insignificant left and walked for a couple of meters. He knocked at the dreary door. It was unlocked. He got down the flight of stairs and entered an alley. Down the alley, behind a closed garage was Night Queen. The place was well lit, bustling with activity. No one wore masks, no social distancing. It seemed as though COVID was happening in some other world.

Sandeep went and met Rocker, the slang name of the person on the betting table. Sandeep gave him a stack of dollars and said with caution, "This better work." He held Rocker's hand as he gave the money to him, as though pleading to make him win. Rocker winked. The game started. 9,6,3,1 -   and the winning number was 5. Sandeep had lost the bet yet again and with it, the last few dollars left with him. He wiped the perspiration from his forehead and nervously scratched his beard. He didn't know what to do.

Sandeep had tried to get rid of his betting habit. But, the current economic crisis had just added to the fuel. Shailaja paid him enough for his work. But, his wrongdoings had caused him heavy losses. As a result, he was in a lot of debt. He knew well that if he asked for more money from Shailaja, she would send him to the police. Being a benevolent lady, she had already helped him many times financially as well as personally. She was not getting her salary for six months now. He was ashamed to ask her for more.

But, there was no money to even put food on their plates in a family of four.

Sandeep had illegally migrated to California from Palestine. 'Sandeep' – his name was also fake. He, along with his wife and two kids, came to California looking for a brighter and stable future.

Shailaja saw him working in the hospital as a sanitation worker. They spoke for some time. She offered him an additional job as house help, which Sandeep gladly accepted.

Now, with the hospital job not paying salaries and his betting debts growing, he had come to his wit's end as to how to provide for his family. He cursed himself for doing this to his family. In frustration, he banged his head on the wall.

BANGGG!

The noise was heard by Dev who was patrolling the area on night duty.
At this time of the day, the work of police personnel was only to ensure that no killings happen. They let all the other activities of Night Queen proceed amicably.
Dev saw Sandeep's wounded head and confronted him.
"What's up buddy?" "You seem undone."
"I have seen you somewhere. Oh yes, you are Shailaja's driver, right?"
Sandeep did not utter a word. He was scared.

Dev took Sandeep for a walk with him. Sandeep could not help but reveal that he had no money. He was a refugee in California. He had a family to support and huge debts to pay. Dev felt bad for him. He warned him and let him go, but made a mental note of the occurrence. Shailaja needs to be informed.

Chapter 12

Solidarity Trial

WHO launched the Solidarity Trial for research in the field of COVID 19 treatment and vaccine development on March 18th,2020. As of July 1st,2020, 5500 patients in 21 countries had been recruited for the trial.

The funding for the trial reached the US $ 108 million from individual donations, charitable organizations, and 45 participating countries' government contributions.

The treatment trial intended to rapidly assess in thousands of COVID 19 infected people the efficacy of existing antiviral and anti-inflammatory agents, not yet evaluated specifically for COVID 19 illness, a process called 'repurposing' or 'repositioning' an already approved drug for a different disease.

The Solidarity trial is designed to give rapid insight about key clinical questions like:
- Mortality rates
- Duration of hospitalization
- Need for ventilation and ICU care
- Effect of prophylaxis in health care workers

Drugs under the study included:
- Remdesivir
- Lopinavir / Ritonavir combined
- Interferon-beta combined with Lopinavir
- Hydroxychloroquine (HHCQ) (discontinued due to no benefit in June 2020).

In October 2020, the WHO Solidarity Trial produced an interim report concluding that its Remdesivir, HCQ, Lopinavir, and Interferon regimens appeared to have little or no benefit on hospitalized COVID 19 patients. This conclusion was drawn after studying indicators like overall mortality, initiation of ventilation, and duration of hospital stay.

Gilead – the manufacturer of Remdesivir, criticized the Solidarity Trial methodology.

Solidarity Trial for vaccine candidates:

WHO established a multinational coalition of scientists for the development of a vaccine for coronavirus disease. WHO defined Global Target Product Profile (TPP) for COVID 19. This team identified favorable attributes of safe and effective vaccines for two categories of people:

- Vaccines for people at high risk of infection like health care workers
- Vaccines to provide rapid response limiting catastrophic new outbreaks

The participating countries were ensured fast interpretation and sharing of results around the world. This would facilitate the ease of Phase II and III trials and uniform protocols to roll out the vaccine when it arrives, with systematic community distribution worldwide.

Chapter 13

The Volunteer

Shailaja had been told that a candidate vaccine was soon to be put to stage three trials. That would involve human volunteers. Healers Hospital would be a part of the human trials.

A brief meeting for all the hospital staff was convened. Instructions were given, that in addition to their hectic COVID duties, they were now expected to get healthy volunteers enrolled for the vaccine trial. The early birds would get attractive bonuses. There was a price for every human life. People would be subjected to a candidate vaccine with unknown benefits and side effects. The money would be paid to attract them to barter their health.

All the gory images of guinea pigs being used as research animals appeared in the minds of the attendees in the meeting. But, they were given a target to meet. So, everyone buckled up and went about their newfound role of vaccine subject hunters. Shailaja was baffled. She was not willing to be a part of the subject hunting crew. She was not sure if the trial had been approved by the ethics committee of the hospital. But the, it was not up to her to decide. The trial was on.

Such was the circle of life. For generations to benefit, those surviving today were meant to sacrifice, discover, build, and evolve, only to get extinct and give way to a further era of creatures.
Was it a good time to be a human being? I guess any time is fine to be a good human being.

Shailaja knew that Sandeep was going through a very tough time. His reality was much worse than any imagination. The family had no income, no food on their plates, no roof over their heads. Fear of debts, refugee status, and COVID, loomed large over their minds.

Shailaja told Sandeep about the vaccine trial and the cash that was being offered. Sandeep happily accepted the offer. It seemed like a godsend option for him in such stressed times. Shailaja explained to him every detail about the side effects that she knew but that information just went off the roof for Sandeep. He was elated by

the shining opportunity about which he had just
become privy to.

Chapter 14

<u>Vaccine Trials Elsewhere</u>

In another part of the world, Korea, COVID vaccine trials were in an advanced stage. But, the vaccine could not see the light of the day. 45 volunteers were registered for the trial. 19 of them suffered sudden death due to unknown reasons.

Multiple opinions were afloat in the media. Was the trial hurried due to extensive pressure and competition between countries and world organizations to come up first with a vaccine? Were safety and ethical norms flouted?

Being able to develop a vaccine for coronavirus would be a matter of great pride and honor for any country, and also a huge economic opportunity.

Every country in the world was hit badly by the pandemic. The health of the citizens was doomed, the economy went crashing. Huge losses were incurred and even more, were predicted for the next quarter. The year 2020 had proved to be a game-changer for many – some won, most lost.

In this vivid scenario, China was able to control the pandemic and restrict it to the province of Hubei. Even adjoining provinces like Henan, Anhui, and Jiangxi, reported only sporadic cases. No large clusters were noted.

The daily number of active cases of coronavirus in China was highest on February 11th, 2020 at 6905. Thereafter, it dipped to 16 on March 15th and has remained such ever since. On November 25th, active cases in a day were 21.

Many countries of the world, especially America blamed China for introducing coronavirus to the world and causing such a huge calamity. They suspected that China already had a vaccine and also probably a cure for the disease. That is how they were able to control the pandemic in China while spreading it to the rest of the world. China must be held responsible for millions of deaths worldwide. The actions were equated to World War III by some in the media.

WHO's intentions were also held suspicious by several countries, which stated that the WHO took China's side and did not reveal complete information about the disease in time. This led to the spread of the virus and disease becoming uncontrollable with community transmission.

More such rumors did rounds in the media and news channels regularly. The mind was fret with negativity, allegations, and malicious intents – only to realize that probably none of them or all of them were true. Who knows????

Chapter 15

Guinea Pig fails

Sandeep enrolled in the vaccine trial. The day he went for his first dose, his wife sent him away with tears of hope in her eyes. Sandeep was happy that finally, something positive was happening in their lives, and this time he was not bringing them misery or fear, but hope and happiness. He had never felt so proud to be himself, just his being.

At the Healers hospital, he was taken to the vaccination facility. The paramedics brought a chic looking casket, opened it with caution, tool out a greenish pre-loaded syringe, and injected Sandeep. He winced. It was nothing compared to the happiness in his wife's eyes.

He returned home and his regular job. This cycle repeated over the next two months for two more booster shots at 30-day intervals. Sandeep was doing fine. The cash from the vaccine trial ensured that their financial woes were ameliorated temporarily. He paid off the debts in part with his savings and finally, things started improving.

He enrolled himself for propaganda during the coming US presidential elections, again to earn few easy dollars. They had to walk all day with banners in their hands. It was a bright and sunny day. Spirits were high. Slogans were being chanted. Blue flags of the democratic party unfurled all along the way.

After the day was over and the evening sun started setting, Sandeep felt a jolt or shiver in his spine. The fellow people noticed him twitching. In a matter of a few seconds, his whole body went into a spasm. His teeth were clenched. Froth was coming out of his mouth, eyes rolled up. He could not control his limbs. He urinated in his pants and then, the world went numb.

Shailaja got Sandeep admitted as her relative. Any other way would not be possible to get medical attention for a refugee – and that too in the COVID scenario. The fact that he was enrolled in the vaccine trial helped a bit.

Sandeep's family was very thankful to Shailaja for all her help, initially enrolling Sandeep in the vaccine trial and getting rid of their financial troubles, and now helping him in getting treated for seizures. Sandeep was conscious and taking food orally. However, the episode left him paraplegic, that is, both his lower limbs had no use now. He could not walk. He was wheelchair-bound. The doctors said that it was a temporary thing. The infection would settle and Sandeep would recover. But, Sandeep's mind caved in. it spiraled deep down into the ravines of depression.

Weeks passed and there was no improvement in Sandeep's condition. His wife tried to help him out but he vented out his aggression on her. Unable to cope with hungry faces, his wife started a part-time job as a house help. This was the final nail in the coffin of Sandeep's ego as a man. He could not provide for his family and now, his wife was forced to work in other people's houses to make ends meet. He began blaming himself for all the miseries.

Shailaja used to visit Sandeep regularly in the hospital. She was privy to some facts that nobody else knew and she was not proud of it. Viral meningitis leading to infarcts and paralysis was a dreaded side effect of the COVID vaccine, mentioned in small letters so that no one would read it. Sandeep was the first one to manifest such symptoms. Although she did not let it show on her face, she silently took the guilt of introducing him to the trial.

And then it happened. She had just entered the ward where Sandeep was admitted. She heard an ominous "THUD". She went running to the window. Out of the window of the 18th-floor ward, she stuck her neck out and saw Sandeep's lifeless body lying in a pool of blood on the sidewalk on the ground below. Sandeep had committed suicide to relieve himself of all his guilt and miseries.

Chapter 16

The Troubled Dove

Shailaja went to Patel's room. Patel had contracted COVID in November and was now on the path of recovery. He got admitted to the Healers hospital in a private ward.

His illness had proven to be a blessing in disguise for their relationship. Patel caught hold of the missing block in the puzzle of his life. COVID made him realize that there is no tomorrow. He understood the importance of life, the value of health, and happiness like never before.

You don't need an excess of money around you to be happy. You just need the unconditional love of your near and dear ones and basic amenities to enjoy life. This revelation dawned on him a little late, but 'better late than never'.

He decided that he would propose to Shailaja today and had kept ready a ring for the same. Although a private ward in a hospital was not the ideal place to propose your love, so be it. It had to be done today.

When Shailaja entered the room, Patel smiled with joy. But, his jaw dropped and his smile vanished when he saw the look on Shailaja's face. She sat beside him and burst into tears. This was most unexpected from a lady whom everyone in the community had begun to admire and respect for her selfless service and calm attitude in times of COVID.

"What happened?"
Shailaja told him that Sandeep committed suicide and she held herself responsible for the miseries he was subjected to. How would she face his wife now?

This is what happens to people who are good at heart and great at intellect. Their endeavors to be right and just at all times, sometimes gets them trapped in their self-guilt for tasks that were aimed to help others. So, should we not even try to help others? Is extending a helping hand a detrimental effort?

No, no.

Devdutt Patnaik in his book "The Seven Secrets of Vishnu" states that only man in the realm of nature has been given the function of brain and intellect. Only man can change the jungle law where 'Might is right' and 'Survival of the fittest' pervades. The human existence ensues from divine culture through ages and generations where strong help the meek. So long as we follow the jungle law, we are 'pashu' or animals. Only when we rise above it and start establishing 'dharma', do we become worthy of being human.

So, every action of Shailaja was justified. All she needed at this time was a shoulder to cry on, a hand to hold so that her agitated feelings could get some rest. Though not the perfect time, Patel took out the box of the ring from under his pillow and kept it in front of Shailaja. Wiping her tears, Shailaja looked at it. She understood what it was. Patel's eyes were filled with hope and love for her.

She regained her composure and said, "I guess I need to welcome someone in my life. Thank you

and YES!" and hugged Patel. Patel hugged her back tightly. She had never felt so good in any man's arms till now in her life. It was a surreal feeling like she had arrived at her destination. True love is beyond the boundaries of words, or languages, or age, or differences. It is only felt, deep inside the heart.
'When true love comes, there is but one.'

Chapter 17

Living with coronavirus

In November, 2020, New York Times ran an
article
'Coping with coronavirus – how the world is
gradually learning to live with COVID 19.

Around the world, the governments appeared to
accept the coronavirus and are adjusting to the
reality that the disease is here to stay. But, there
is a shift in strategy from damaging nationwide
lockdowns to targeted ways to find and stop
outbreaks before they turn into the second wave
of the pandemic.

The details differ with location and
administration, but the strategies remain a mix
of intensive testing and monitoring, lightning-
fast response time by authorities, tight border
management, and constant reminders to citizens
for self-discipline, social distancing, cough
etiquette and mask hygiene.

COVID scenario has forced central and local governments to work closely together overlooking turf battles and bureaucratic rivalries. Most of the successful countries cannot declare victory against COVID until a vaccine is found. In countries like the United States of America, Brazil, India, the initial outbreak could never be fully contained.

"It is always going to be with us," said Simon James Thornley, an epidemiologist for the University of Auckland in New Zealand. "I don't think we can eliminate the virus long term. We are going to need to learn to live with the virus."

A tobacco shop owner in Japan commented, "As soon as we lower our guard, it bites us back. We have to remain careful forever." It took us a pandemic to generate this kind of general awareness towards health and hygiene. It is a big price for humanity to pay.

South Korea calls its strategy as 'everyday life quarantine'. It does not enforce strict lockdown. But, strongly encourages social distancing. It has set itself a target of 50 new infections a day, a target that its public health system can withstand with testing and tracing capability. It has advised people to carry two types of masks: a surgical mask and a heavy-duty mask, similar to N95 respirator masks worn by health care workers, to be used in crowded settings.

Citizens worldwide are expected to avoid 3 Cs – closed, crowded, and close contact activities.

Britain Prime Minister Boris Johnson likened the approach to 'Whac a mole' – identify local outbreaks, take measures on the spot, rather than go back to nationwide lockdown approach.

All over the world, people had realized that initial lockdowns were only for the re-appropriation of resources. The strategy now depended on public motivation to maintain the health and hygiene of self and others in the community. Being responsible and dedicated to join the government's efforts to abate the pandemic was the only way out. Standing in solidarity with humanity was the need of the hour – like never before.

Many NGOs (non-governmental organizations) got together to help people with food and water, transportation to reach their homes, helped

them with alternative skills when they lost their
regular jobs.

But, still, the pandemic was very much there.
The future unknown – the guards could not be
laid down – that was the truth.

And at that moment, it struck. The world would
never be the same again.

Chapter 18

The adjustments

The COVID scenario continued unabated.

Angad and Shruti's marriage missed many 'shubh muhurats' as Shailaja was busy with her commitments at the hospital. Angad and Shruti decided that they will have a court marriage. This would involve less number of people. The government regulations entailed that only fifty people could attend a marriage ceremony and attendees at a funeral would be limited to twenty only. Shailaja however, wanted an extravagant function for her only son.

Angad and Shruti did not want to wait anymore. There was no likely end to the COVID pandemic. The vaccine was expected, but efficacy could not be guaranteed. There was no timeline in sight. Life had to move on.

Angad and Shruti took their cups of tea and brought one for Shailaja too. They sat at the dining table with biscuits in their hands. The look on their faces revealed their thoughts. "Ma, let's have a simple wedding ceremony. A court marriage would do. We can plan a formal reception later." Angad looked at Shailaja expectantly.

"Sure. That's a fine idea. I also wanted to share something with both of you." Shailaja placed her hand on Angad and Shruti's and told them that she had accepted Patel's hand in marriage.

"We are so happy for you Maa. We have been waiting for this so long!" said Angad.

Shailaja was astonished. It seemed that it was just her in the house who was not privy to what was cooking. Anyways, all were happy now and hugged each other.

Chapter 19

The D day

Today was another auspicious day. Ten months after their engagement, Angad and Shruti were finally getting married. Amongst family and friends, they exchanged the customary 'varmala', and Angad placed the sacred 'mangalsutra' around Shruti's neck. They signed on the marriage register and were pronounced man and wife.

"Congratulations!!!"

The couple could not plan a honeymoon as international flights had not yet restarted. So, they planned a 'staycation' at a nearby hotel. Hotels and restaurants had just been opened a month back with strict COVID precautions. This was a welcome getaway for people from their mundane routines.

Today was special for one more reason. Another wedding was scheduled. Shailaja and Patel also tied the knot at the same setting.

The family photo had everyone wearing masks – the masked memories, but not the emotions.

Happiness and relationships returned to the household in times of tumultuousness and calamity – a perfect example of finding positives among all negatives.

Life goes on. The human race, homo sapiens sapiens, have an indomitable spirit, an insatiable thirst to EXIST. In an atmosphere where death, sickness, and miseries were abounding, Shailaja's family found unlimited happiness, newfound love, and stability. Such was the design of the human race, to rise like a phoenix from its ashes.

Dev, the sheriff, and Sandeep's wife also attended the function. In a quiet talk, Dev revealed to Shailaja that the information of Sandeep being involved in a vaccine trial was successfully erased from all records. If this information would have leaked, Shailaja's reputation, Sandeep's wife's refugee status problems, and the vaccine trial itself – all would get in jeopardy. Sandeep's wife would not be able to get a job easily if her refugee status was revealed.

Dev ensured that Sandeep's wife got all her paperwork done in time and also secured a reasonable job for her in a community eating joint.

Shailaja thanked Dev for all the help. Dev waived off his hand in his customary style and said, "Hey! That's what friends are for. Anyways, I just completed the good job that you intended to do."

31 December 2020

Patel came to the Nursing College in his new swanky car to pick up Shailaja. Shailaja had taken retirement from the Healers Hospital and joined a nursing college. The administration at the college was more than happy when she accepted their offer as the Head of Training. They had been pursuing Shailaja for many years. Shailaja thought that now was a good time to take a less stressful job and enjoy life before it's too late.

She worked with the Healers Hospital for eight months during COVID. These eight months, she had put her health, her mind, and her love, everything at stake. Her anxiety levels had skyrocketed. Her panic attacks had increased.

Finally, Patel and Angad counseled her to be a little kind to herself.

Shailaja was sent off from the Healers Hospital with a quiet farewell. Everyone acknowledged her contributions to patients' health and wished her well for her future endeavors.

Shailaja joined the nursing college and was very happy to train enthusiastic young students. Being among fresh students is a different kick altogether. You get to shape young minds. It is a huge responsibility.

Today was Shailaja and Patel's turn to get vaccinated. VACCINAC – the COVID vaccine had just been launched into the market after going through all trials. Being a part of the health sector, Shailaja and her family were vaccinated in the first swing. An apt day for vaccination as the new year approaches.

2021 is expected to bring some relief to the miseries across the world, light, and spirit to the human race.

Chapter 20

The Prelude

November 23, 2020

Excerpts from an English daily review feature.

The origin of COVID 19 disease – Lab or wet market?

The year 2020 showed the world a pandemic, the coronavirus disease or COVID 19, that infected 58.6 million people worldwide and caused 1.39 million deaths.

The origin of the novel coronavirus outbreak remains a mystery, with experts having different views on whether the virus came from a laboratory or a seafood wet market in the city of Wuhan, China.

While the scientific community has concluded that the virus is natural and not man-made or genetically modified, the possibility that the virus escaped from a laboratory in Wuhan remains.

US Secretary of State, Mike Pompeo, stated that there was "enormous evidence" that the coronavirus emerged from a Chinese laboratory. Other US officials and analysts state that the virus either escaped from a Wuhan government laboratory or was introduced through human contact with wildlife at a market in Wuhan city. In any version, China was the origin of this calamity and yet, it was not among the worst affected regions. This scenario was suspicious.

In midst of all this mayhem, World Health Organization (WHO), the body expected to deal with the pandemic in action, not advisory capacity, also echoed Chinese sentiments that the virus originated in animals.

The public has yet to see definitive proof of the origin of coronavirus. Worldwide scientific deliberations have shifted from the origin of the virus to vaccine development and disease prevention. Chances are that this mystery may remain unsolved forever. Whatever theories are known today, are all likelihood scenarios. We will never know for sure. We can only speculate.

US Office of the Director of National Intelligence, which oversees the country's intelligence agencies and organizations, stated that it agreed with the consensus that the COVID 19 virus was not man-made. However, it would continue to examine whether a normal virus was accidentally released from a laboratory in China. The lab in question is the Wuhan Institute of Virology. It was visited by officials of the US State department in 2018. Safety concerns were then raised and the institute was warned that it had the potential to cause a SARS-like pandemic, according to a Washington Post report.

Chinese authorities also prevented foreign virologists and epidemiologists from participating in the investigation of the epidemic.

Meanwhile, medical journals carried reports, some of which supported the Wuhan sea market origin, while others supported the lab leak origin. The Chinese government explicitly

accepted the preliminary scientific dictum that
Wuhan wet market was linked to the outbreak.
Yet, the first COVID patient – the zero case –
had no exposure to the market.

All these and more, linked and difficult
questions remained unanswered as the world
entered the New Year. Festivities of Christmas
and New Year were knocking on the doors.

Chapter 21

<u>*What did we learn in 2020?*</u>

The year that was, taught us all many things. The few take-aways from this memoir are appended below:

1. Value time. The rising of the sun in the morning and the light of the moon should never be taken for granted.

   If you have an appointment or a meeting, reach in time. If you are late, the other person doesn't need to be also like you. Respect time and you will be rewarded. Everyone in this world has 24 hours in a day. But the success of each person varies according to the way they manage their time. People commonly complain that they couldn't get something done as they didn't have time for it. In reality, they did have time, but, they spent it loitering away or doing useless things.

2. Value the love and friendship of your near and dear ones. That is something you would not want to live without.

When a person is asked what his basic needs are, most of the time the answer is "Roti, kapda aur makaan"(food, clothes, and shelter). People forget that man is a social animal and having friends and relatives comes naturally to him. Loving and caring for others gives meaning and purpose to our life. Love and relationships give us identity. Studies mention that if a person does not love anyone in the world, he is at high risk for depression and suicide. Detachment from everything is a trait of sages, not normal human beings.

Love unconditionally. There is just one life. If you are lucky enough to get hold of your true love, the ONE, do not let it pass you by. Keep it with you, treasured, forever and ever.

3. Work is worship. Ask the jobless person how he wished to remain busy.

    Working keeps us busy, challenges us, and gives us the means to develop ourselves. It gives us a sense of pride, identity, and personal achievement. It enables us to socialize, build contacts, and find support. It provides us with money to support ourselves and explore our interests. People at work tend to enjoy happier and healthier lives than those who are not at work. Our physical and mental health is generally improved through work – we recover from sickness quicker and are at less risk of long term illness and incapacity.

4. Money cannot buy health.

    WHO defines health as "The complete state of physical, mental and social well-being, and not merely the absence of disease or infirmity".

Your health is your best companion. And you and only you, are responsible for it. So, make conscious choices. Do not be swayed by peer pressure.

5. Money is important for living. So, save for your future.

    Money is an essential commodity that helps you run your life. Money has gained its value because people are trying to save wealth for their future needs. Philosophically speaking, money cannot buy everything but practically money is the basic thing that is used for survival in this world.

    Money is a good servant but a bad master.

    You should be fond of money to an extent that you are controlling it. Don't fall into the evil hands of money. If you are a lavish spender, spending money in unnecessary ways, you will soon lose all your wealth. Hard work and commitment is essential if you want money to stay in your hands.

If you have money, signs of poverty will never approach you and you can maintain your health, but not rule your health.

You should use the money for solving your financial problems but you should be careful that your money does not transform you into a different person. If you earn truckloads of money, and by your swaggering attitude turn away your loved ones, that kind of money will never contribute to your happiness.

6. The world order may change at any time.

Patriotism can be defined as the love of one's country, identification with it, and special concern for its well-being.

Staying in a wealthy country does not ensure your happiness. Love your motherland.

7. Value nature and simple joys of life.

The trees, the birds, the wind, the dewdrops – all this is your gift when you

are born. Enjoy them, but do take good
care of them.

The simple things in life that give you joy,
do them today. A leisurely walk, gossip
with friends, hugging your children –
these activities do not cost money. Do
them often to keep yourself sane.

8. Mental health is as important as physical health.

Give your mind a relaxing massage as you
would do to your body in a spa. Do not
take stress. Talk to people. Make friends.

Mental health includes emotional,
psychological, and social well-being. It
affects how we think, feel, and act. It also
helps determine how we handle stress,
relate to others, and make choices.
Mental health is important at every stage
of life, from childhood and adolescence
through adulthood.

During your life, if you experience mental
health problems, your thinking, mood,
and behavior could be affected. Before
these effects become detrimental, take
action, and reach out.

Speaking out openly about a mental issue has never been easy. But there is no other way to sort it out. It is imperative to open up to a friend, counselor, or healer to deal with your issues. Let's face it!

9. Have faith.

Life is beautiful, but, undoubtedly, it can be filled with difficult and even unbearable moments. During seasons of loss and emptiness, there may seem like there is no way of breaking through, whether you're grappling with the death of a loved one, or heartbreak, or your lowest trough. In these tough times, faith can make a difference.

If you know of a friend who needs a little positivity or you're searching for strength yourself, sharing compassion and positivity always helps.

Whoever you are, whatever work you do, there is a higher force that drives you towards your purpose in the universe.

Faith sees the invisible, believes the unbelievable, and delivers the impossible.

10.Live, survive.

There are times in eternity when you are bestowed with all positive tracks and turns, you make the best decisions, ultimate choices, and harness the energy of the universe completely. You become a success story and a force to reckon with. Your time!

At other times, there is despair, calamity, sadness. You are unable to rise even when you are working hard. You fall sick. You fall, get depressed. You lose your purpose in life.

This cycle of events may alternate or occur in our lives in any combination. But, remember to live through them. Take the pain, take the acclaim in a balanced way.

Success should not rise to your head and neither should failure depress you. Just survive them. For, in the long run, you will witness the wonders of life. There is one life given to everyone. Live it to the fullest and witness the magic. Claim your luck. Strengthen your mind to fight with any adversity. Think high, live with simplicity.

With these principles, let us pledge that we will not let the pandemic rise above humankind. Together, we shall rise, rise again, and rebuild, all that has been lost, with love, with hope.

Chapter 22

The Conclusion

"And just as the phoenix rose from the ashes,
  She too will rise.
  Returning from the flames clothed in nothing
but her strength
  More beautiful than ever before."
  -   SHANNEN HEARTZS

What happened in the year 2020, defied all definitions of normal. It was the other extreme. It was all terms negative and chaotic like mayhem, adversity, disaster, PANDEMIC.

The world order was about to change. The generation that lived and did not die in COVID 19 would have horrific tales to tell. This book is one such account.

Human beings are thought to have originated 160,000 years ago. This tribe has faced and lived

through innumerable adversities and continues
to evolve, with hope at the core of its existence.

In life sometimes, we reach a point of no return,
a point where there is no way forward. When we
reach that point, everything seems still, silent.
The year 2020 was one such point. Now, what
we can do is quietly accept the fact and move
ahead. That's how we survive. With strength,
with acceptance, with love.

I have seen better days
But, I have seen worse.
I don't have everything that I want,
But, I do have all I need.
I wake up with some aches and pains, but, I
wake up.
To a new day, to a new life, to some new hope.
My life may not be perfect,
But, I know I am blessed.
And I will not let go, of hope, of life.
    -    Lessons learned in life.

References:

This being my fact-based memoir on the COVID 19 pandemic, I would like the reader to know the source material for this book for further readings:

- WHO Official site
- Ministry of Health and family welfare – corona related information
- Journal articles related to coronavirus
- Interviews with health care workers
- First-hand experience in the pandemic as a health care worker

Full forms of abbreviations used in the book

- WHO – World Health Organization
- OT – Operation Theatre
- ER – emergency room
- NICU – Neonatal Intensive Care Unit
- PPE – personal protective equipment

Did you like the book?

Dear reader,

In the words of Walter Lipmann, "Music is nothing if it falls on deaf ears."

I firmly believe in the fact that the audience gives any artist all that he or she needs.

At this point in my author journey, I crave audience applaud.

Do write your feedback and review about the book at Amazon.

I promise to reach out to every one of you.

This is the first book in the series, "Wholesome Health". Look out for my next books in the series. See you till then. Happy reading!

www.ingramcontent.com/pod-product-compliance
Lightning Source LLC
Chambersburg PA
CBHW061400250726